CW01619233

So Daisy´s Really Are Made In Heaven

Second Edition

Nick Burrin

So Daisy's Really Are Made In Heaven

Second Edition 2021

Nick Burrin Publishing

First Edition was published in 2010

Text Copyright © Nick Burrin 2021

Front Cover Painting and Design © Nick Burrin

All rights reserved. No part of this publication may be reproduced, stored in a retrieval system, or transmitted in any form or by any means, electronic, mechanical, photocopy, recording or otherwise, without prior written permission of the copyright owner. Nor can it be circulated in any form of binding or cover other than that in which it is published and without similar condition including this condition being imposed on a subsequent purchaser.

British Library Cataloguing Publication Data.
A catalogue record for this book is available from the British Library

ISBN 978-0-9955240-8-8

This book is also available in e-book format, details of which are available at www.nickburrin.com

Contents

Introduction

I wake up and feel my hands to see if I still exist. I do, and I wasn't dreaming.

I've always felt my life has been different but I never thought that something like this would ever happen to me. It's like being in a fairy tale, or an imaginary dream – but this is Reality.

Over the past few years my life and awareness has changed. I always thought there must be much more to life than what we all see – but how to connect, how to get in touch with the deeper, inner self.

There has to be one Truth, one Ultimate Knowledge. One everlasting and totally understandable definition of life, of where we have come from, where we are going, and what has created us. What is our relationship with this Awesome Power of Creation.

I realised that nobody really had any concrete answers, because if they did, the world would not have the problems that it now faces. There were many unanswered questions in my mind. Why is there so much pain and suffering. Is it man made. How can we solve the problems that we seem to have created. How can we improve. How do we find peace. Are all the answers really much closer than we think. Is there some way we can change, move on, elevate our lives into new perceptions of discrimination and individual benevolence. Perhaps there is a new level of consciousness yet to be discovered.

I seem to have the most enormous amount of energy and power. My days have changed and I have gone beyond time. My body only needs three to four hours sleep a night. I can't seem to think about sleeping or eating at all, they seem unimportant. This is such a beautiful thing that is happening to me, and it's so difficult to put into words. It's happening to me most of the day now and I pray that it doesn't stop. It's just incredible, beyond all human expectation. I could never have believed anything like this could ever take place.

What's in store for all of us is just phenomenal.

Nick Burrin

Chapter 1

The Awakening

Sunday night, Abi's house, London, June 1994
(Handwritten)
I'm going to try and explain to you a series of experiences that provided answers to all the questions I had ever asked. I go back and forth between the past and present because that is how these events seem to have been taking place.

It all started late one summer evening. I was sitting with my friend Abi and we were talking about relationships between people. As we spoke, I began to feel elated, that love was unconditional and everlasting, and that it is possible to love everyone and everything. My heart was opening. I was filled with joy and bliss, and the music was so soothing. Suddenly a light appeared through the front door, entered the room and turned into a Divine Personality.

A Mother, a beautiful Mother. The Primordial Mother.

Mother is everywhere, sitting in the armchair, towering over the house. The room is filled with Angels and there are Deities bowing at Mother's Feet. My body feels light, without any stress or strain, as if I am disconnected from it. The top of my head has opened, I feel completely in the moment and totally connected to Heaven. Inside me are waves of eternal joy, I feel part of the whole. There is light pouring from The Primordial Mother into my heart and from my heart into Abi's heart and then back to mine again.

There is a frenzy of activity and movement, and the roof of the house has opened. There is light pouring out of the house, and it is no longer on the earth, as if it is ascending to Heaven. There are Angels moving up and down the spiral staircase and the staircase seems to go on forever. They are dressed in white, pure and innocent, transparent, and They are so beautiful.

My body feels insignificant. I don't feel human, but ancient and eternal. My attention feels very powerful, as if it can transform. I am lost in a timeless space. I feel small, humble, clean and pure. Completely clear, absolutely cleansed. The music playing on the stereo is penetrating right through me, as if every note is being played inside me, connecting me to the Universe.

Mother is smiling at me. Mother has closed Mother's Eyes and has gone into meditation. I can feel this Eternal Mothering Energy inside me, and then coming out of the top of my head like a Bright Light. Mother is asking us to go somewhere, but I don't know where. I feel goodness and beauty in everyone I think of, as if God has been awakened in all of them.

There are so many things I want to communicate, but I can't talk. I don't feel the need to talk any more in this state. It is difficult to imagine a world where everyone is in this Consciousness. It will happen. I can't express in words what that feels like.

I see my whole life before me.
I see my past,
The beauty of life and happiness.
In this state,
I can feel everything about everyone,
I can go anywhere.

Travel the world with my attention.
All that I feel,
All that I experience,
My whole awareness moves
To verify my realisation.
My attention has the power of light
The Light of The Mother
Awesomely penetrating and cleansing.
Everything can be done for us,
If only we surrender.

Suddenly I feel free. Rules have ceased to exist, and all the old conditionings of life are vanishing. There is no time or limitations. No anxiety, just new dimensions of existence. What are human qualifications, without Divine Intuition and Divine Connection. In this Consciousness I feel immortal, ever young and getting younger.

Age and old age don't exist any more. Ageing is just another conditioning. There is no fear, only fear in other people. God has everything and desires nothing. It is a strange world we have created, of conformity. There is now only one way forward but it seems a tall order. I feel I am turning into light now. It doesn't feel frightening. In this state there are no problems, only solutions. I look in the mirror but I don't see myself.

There is no doubt that life will ever be the same again. Nothing is more important than devoting time to experience what is happening to me, although I feel it will be difficult to exist in two lives – but I know The Divine Mother will help me.

Reflecting on that night, I realise that for some years, I had an overwhelming desire welling inside me to tangibly understand the truth about life. And then – here I am, still

Nick, still leading a normal existence, yet whenever I desired, I could go into this new-found experience of Awareness and Consciousness. As if it was a gift from Creation itself.

Chapter 2

Expectation

Sunday 3rd July 1994, West Bay Beach, Dorset
(Handwritten)
Over the next few days, the experiences subsided a little. But every so often, The Divine Mother would appear and there would be Angels around us. It wasn't until the following weekend that I had another really strong experience.

We'd gone to Dorset for the weekend, to enjoy the sun and the sea. On the Sunday morning, I drove with Abi down to West Bay Beach.

Abi and I wandered down the beach, walking in amongst the families and children playing. It was nice to feel the sand between our toes. We found a nice spot and as I sat down on the sand, I realised that something very powerful was about to happen.

I surrender to The Will of God,
The Power of the Cosmos.
Divinity is gathering,
Coming across the sea
To this place, to rejoice.
Angels are coming from every direction,
In anticipation of Mother arriving,
Rejoicing in my new-found connection.

Once again, Mother arrives. A man I recognise also appears. It is William Blake. William Blake is now sitting on my left. Coming from William Blake is this tremendous feeling of depth and expression. Mother is facing me seated on a beautiful carved chair.

Music is playing in the background. Once again I am in this timeless, beautiful place. Everything is moving very quickly and I feel something is about to happen. Then I look out to sea and the sea turns into a wise eternal grandfather. Mother turns to me and asks me to forgive, to unfold the limits of my mind. And then out of my head a white burst of light to The Heavens. My head is once again open.

I ask Mother for answers, for Divine Inspiration, and a Hand comes out of the sky and pours nectar on the beach. I feel I am being elevated to new heights. Mother is seated with weapons all around Mother. Mother is now turning into Lord Shiva, The Deity behind the creation, destruction and re-creation of the Universe. The Primordial Mother is knighting me with a spear in some kind of ceremony on the beach, perhaps preparing me for battle.

Shri Ganesha appears, The Elephant-headed Eternal Child, and the music inspires Shri Ganesha to dance, so beautifully and delicately. All The Angels stop to watch. Shri Ganesha is suddenly awesome, one hundred feet high, walking out of the sea. Shri Ganesha shrinks and dissolves into Mother and They are now one, sitting as Mother as Shri Ganesha.

Mother has no real face, a sign of The Final Coming. The end is nigh. A fresh beginning. Inside, I am desiring answers. What should I do. Simply experience Heaven on Earth. I feel the world is evolving and changing, and suddenly it is as if I am above, looking down on England. England is turning into

Lord Shiva and Lord Shiva sits up, as in the words of William Blake: 'Awaken O' sleeping Albion, awaken'.

A massive battle is raging all around us. The Angels draw huge swords. I knew this was pending. Mother's Attention is on my heart, Mother tells me not to fear, and as the battle continues all around us, Mother goes into complete meditation. Mother is not disturbed. Perhaps this means that when we have problems, we should just be silent in meditation, and they will be solved. The battle then subsides and Mother changes into a beautiful young girl and Angels are sprinkling rose petals all around us.

I suddenly hear a baby crying on the beach, and as I turn around, an Angel swoops down and soothes the baby, who stops crying. England, The Heart of the Universe, has awakened and peace is spreading across the Earth.

Lord Jesus Christ has arrived out of the sea. Lord Jesus is a big man, not what I had imagined. Very strong and powerful, with large arms and big strong calf muscles and legs. Completely different to the church's image. Lord Jesus bows to The Divine Mother and sits next to Mother.

Suddenly, just as quickly as it began, this Divine Experience is over. Everyone has gone. I feel it is a test, to see if I fear Them going, fear Them not being there. So I surrender and suddenly They are all back again. Perhaps this is to teach me detachment.

Now, Mother has grown into something too powerful, too much to describe. Six hundred feet high, towering above the beach and Mother's White Saris are the waves breaking on the beach.

Shri Krishna has arrived, playing the Divine Melody on Shri Krishna's Flute. The Earth suddenly turns into a thunderbolt. Mother says Mother has all the answers and I ask what part I should play. Mother replies, "In time, you will know". I feel enormous, like a giant – and then small. I have wings like an Angel. I bow at Mother's Feet and ask if there is any message I should give. Mother says, "Love, just love. Tell people to ask with their hearts".

I wonder if all The Incarnations, Seers and Sages in the world felt so powerful on the one hand and so helpless on the other.

The only way forward for man is the journey into this new Consciousness. But how can we get there with our limited human mind. Perhaps the way forward is through tremendous motivation and joy – the inspiration to motivate man to go beyond his limits and realise his true identity and destiny. To give people the knowledge that there is more to life, that when this Divine Energy is awakened in people, it spontaneously leads to pure joy, and when this energy rises for the first time, it creates, breaks free and lets forth joy. Is this not the moment we all aspire to.

After this experience, a realisation came to me. One of the things we have to face is our tremendous feeling of expectation, which seems to be the cause and destruction of our society. If people were allowed to be themselves, from that would come a sense of dignity and self-respect. Once you have expectations, you create inadequacy and fear. But how do we live without expectations. By grooming the powers of detachment and witnessing. Someone who witnesses is someone who allows.

Without conditionings and expectations, the human will evolve with the qualities of innate Divinity. All the qualities of Divinity, morality, goodness and spontaneity, are within us to be awakened, explored and experienced. But no, the heavy hand of conformity, of tradition for tradition's sake, of fear, severs our natural inborn connection with God. We know it, we have felt it, we have all experienced it. Now all we have to do is realise it. Forgive and forget – move on and upwards.

The only way we can fulfil our potential is by admitting honestly and accepting our mistakes through our limited understanding of this Consciousness. If God had meant us to be slaves, we would have been born with chains. Instead, we have created the chains. So how do we finally unlock ourselves. Let us look at the cause of our problems within ourselves and society. By realising them, we will then have the solutions.

At last, I feel unlimited, released, set free from my own expectations and conditionings.

Life has just begun.

Chapter 3

Joy

Tuesday 5th July 1994, Notting Hill Gate Café, midday

Back here in London, my life has now definitely changed. And what is interesting is that these experiences are completely unnoticed by my friends and other human beings. My friends just say to me, Nick, you look younger, your face looks light and golden, and I just smile. Eternally knowing my immortality.

It is Tuesday and I'm sitting in a café in Notting Hill Gate. At every table and every chair, there are Angels. I suddenly hear music, music I have never heard before, rejoicing once again with this new-found connection. At last, this is Heaven on Earth. How can I be sitting in Notting Hill Gate, yet be in Heaven. Outside, the world moves on with the hustle and bustle of everyday life, I can hear police sirens in the background but The Angels take no notice, They are aware of negativity but They do not register it. They are pure positivity and goodness.

The ceiling is open and the way forth is Heaven. It is a path of light upwards, always beckoning. Another conditioning is on the table. Food. The Angels are asking me to come up with Them. They are saying, "Leave everything behind". The only things that stop me are my human conditionings – how do I let go. They tell me it is just a game and that I will get there. They all smile and bow in acknowledgement and I feel tremendous elation. At this moment, I feel my human body is very tired – They are asking me to rest, but I find it very difficult to rest because I am so excited. I want to share and transmit this new-found joy and connection.

Amidst the jubilation, The Great Mother arrives. The Divine has such a sense of honour. A pure sense of joy that emanates from the heart. I suddenly feel that human jokes are really about mocking and humiliating one another. The important thing about relationships is the strength and not the weakness in the conditioned perception. I feel that we need in every type of relationship, unconditional love. In this new-found Consciousness there is only unconditional love. When your Spirit becomes your mind, it is in direct contact with God. The Truth is what it is.

The words of William Blake keep running through my mind: 'Passion cannot be tamed'. People are always trying to contain us, to put us into boxes, to put labels on us. I understand why William Blake said that 'words fly around the room'. In this new Consciousness everything happens so quickly, and there is a wealth of Pure Knowledge that is being transmitted through me.

I now understand the visions of Blake. The magnitude of Truth and joy I feel, has not really been comprehended by man before. The Truth that remains will destroy the negativity in man. Beware all of those who doubt The Second Coming – time is short, and the message is Resurrection and joy. I look outside and see so many tormented faces. The Divine is pleading with mankind to look upwards, to love, to cherish and to become. The patience of Divinity is enormous.

True art is the surrendering of our ego. There can be no expectation, no gratitude and no material gain, just unconditional surrender for Pure Art to flow. In that State of

Art, if we are humble and completely trusting in our talents, then God will provide for us. I now understand the words 'pennies from Heaven'.

I feel I want to cry and laugh and to jump with joy. Man's spirit needs to be nourished and stimulated through openheartedness with other people. The heart closes and is stifled when we become insular and cut-off from the natural flow of life. Respect between human beings has been lost, if we can regain that respect and protocol then life becomes joyful. We need to understand joy to experience it. Where does joy come from. It comes from open hearts. Joy is love, admitting and accepting. It is the silent bond between human beings, to be awakened and experienced.

How close are joy and sadness to one another. The sadness is the tears but linked to the tears is the joy of realisation. Hence why sadness turns into joy and the clouds turn into sunshine. Pain and suffering all turn into joy if one realises that this is the path to God. Life is all about commitment and respect. It is about conviction and change. As soon as you find a routine, change it. Growth is all about change. It is only fear that makes us stay in a routine.

You only know the right protocol by knowing God. You only know God by meditating on God. Protocol is all built within us innately.

Chapter 4

Introspection

Afternoon 6th July 1994, Nick's flat, London

(Dictaphone)

The next afternoon, I awake from a sleep and The Divine Mother is in Mother's usual chair in my sitting room. Mother smiles. For the first time today, The Divine is gathering. When I go into this state of meditation, Mother appears to me.

Angels begin to appear from all directions in anticipation of this Divine Experience. I look out of the window and see a huge Shri Ganesha walking across London. Shri Ganesha's Enormous Face smiles in through the window. A variety of Divine Beings are bowing at Mother's Feet. I feel tremendous vibrations of cool energy wafting around me, soothing me, increasing this experience to new heights of awareness and meditation. Once again, my head is opening and the path leads to Heaven. There are golden gates lined with Angels. My body feels insignificant, The Angels are pulling at my shirt, inviting me into Heaven. Mother is asking me to go into meditation with Mother.

When one speaks The Truth in this state, The Angels clap, dance and smile. You can always feel The Truth. The Truth is not words, rather, it is felt on your central nervous system. This connection with The Divine is all inspiring, motivating, and so beautiful. It makes one feel as if all our conditionings and problems are so insignificant, and that our economic, social and political problems could be solved in a minute, a whisper, a second.

We need to see our problems, introspect and see where our mistakes lie, to eradicate the negativity within our own human consciousness. The Divine has many Armies, hugely powerful, to destroy that negativity, and the battle will wholeheartedly be won. The negativity within our society will then be destroyed and we will create a beautiful holy place to emancipate humanity, to raise man's consciousness into new heights.

Heaven is amongst us, all around us. I feel an ability to fly amongst the clouds, and at the same time I can feel the sea, the warm wind and spray from the waves, the clouds drifting by. The world is such a beautiful place. I can see the whole Universe smile and turn into The Divine Mother's Face, but of course Mother is the Universe, Mother is Everything and everywhere.

The more I understand The Greatness of God, the more humble I become. That Knowledge of God is the source of our humility. Human ego destroys humility, therefore it must destroy our connection with God. In this state it is so obvious, but sometimes the obvious is hard to see.

Chapter 5

Peace

Monday 11th July 1994, Sierra Nevada, Spain, following a brief thunderstorm

(Handwritten by Abi)

I decided it might be a good idea to leave London, to get away, to go somewhere remote. I decided on Southern Spain, the Sierra Nevada, a beautiful mountain range. I found through some friends a small farm cottage made out of stone. Abi and I drove to Manchester and flew to Spain.

On the flight, I wondered if my experiences would be different. I needed some time to quietly reflect on what was happening to me.

Sitting in the mountains, after a brief thunderstorm, a vision came to me that whoever reads these words, I would humbly request they light a candle in their homes. To bow their heads to the candle, so they would know that the candle flame is the light of their own Spirit. By bowing to the flame, they would enlighten their Spirit, and it would breed a new sense of honour and growth with humility throughout the land. People would then feel The Holy Ghost, The Love of God. This soothing wind or cool breeze of the mountain range would enter their lives and they would realise love in their hearts.

I felt somehow that people could spontaneously receive their Realisation from these words, to bring enlightenment without questioning. The Spirit within us is the flame of the human being. It is important to bow to that flame, unconsciously acknowledging our Spirit.

Suddenly Mother is here, everywhere, and I feel like a rose has opened within us. Perhaps the rose of Spain. A huge gathering is coming to this place. The Virgin Mary is standing over our house. The rocks around me have changed into Shri Ganesha and I feel that the earth is God.

I am now sitting at Mother's Feet and Mother is drawing out the negativity that has been around me for the last few days. Once again, I feel relaxed and humble and I can't find the words to express my thanks to Mother. Now, in this state, I feel a whole new need for expression. To express ourselves through being, through music, art, and through loving.

Our society is so judgmental, every human being feels the need to judge. We are not honest with one another. I see our society is full of misgivings, always analysing. Our words are double-edged and we are scathing. Man needs to aspire to see the qualities and not the imperfections. If we see the qualities in one another, then the imperfections will be destroyed. To feel the qualities in another man is to feel God in another man. God exists within us and the qualities need to be awakened and manifested.

Our society needs to change. Our lives and our work need to be enriched and nourished. The way forward is in nurturing our time and space as individuals. There is an optimum amount of time that we can be constructive and productive. Our maximum working time should be only five to six hours a day. Working more than that leads to stress, anxiety, exhaustion and a breakdown of family and social values. By working less, we would have more time for the truly constructive pursuits.

Time well spent breeds contentment and satisfaction. Our lives, our children, our mothers and fathers, all need time and nourishment. By spending more time with one another, we could enjoy teaching our children to cook, to paint, to swim, to understand and feel nature. If we lived together as a family unit, the grandparents could look after the children, teaching them wisdom and patience, allowing the parents to have time together.

The purpose is to create time and then go beyond it. In this way, we would spend more time in the present and be less worried about the past or the future. Our society would benefit, our minds would be free from stress and our productivity would increase dramatically.

Man can live in peaceful places, but that does not make him peaceful. Man has to have peace within him – then he can live anywhere.

Chapter 6

Faith

Tuesday 12th July 1994, morning, sitting under a tree
I feel I have been around for thousands of years. The knowledge pouring through me is unlimited. As if it is God's Knowledge. Sitting here on the terrace, looking across at the range of mountains, I feel a sense of peace and tranquillity, knowing that the mountain range is an Aspect of God.

The cottage feels as if it has been prepared for this day. The land is levelled, the stage is set, very much like a biblical setting.

Suddenly the Great Mother is here, seated in Mother's chair with numerous Deities bowing before Mother. The magnitude and gravity of the scene deepens now. An enormous gathering of Divine Personalities and Angels are coming to this place. The Mother has gone into meditation. Mother is working on everything, the whole of Spain and the whole of humanity. Mother is asking me to join Mother in meditation and to say a prayer.

I pray to You, Mother,
Mother Of All Mothers,
To take us deeper into ourselves,
To raise the consciousness of man
In achieving his Realisation,
To bring mankind into Your Heart.

We pray that the whole world
Will rejoice in enlightenment,
Please fill us with Your Love,
Divinity and Compassion,
So that we can help each other
Achieve this state of peace and awareness.

As Mother towers above us, all my perspectives are changing and I feel a great shift inside me, surges of realisation. With my entire central nervous system enlightened, I see and feel the gravity of prayer for everyone. Momentarily I feel I have become one with The Divine.

And yet, at the same time, I feel completely humble, without a need for anything. Only trying to come to terms with this enormous realisation, that we can play a part in our own evolution.

I can now see the importance of faith. To have faith in one's self. Faith is knowing that everything will work out. That life is full of twists and turns. The greatest growth in life occurs through times of extreme pain, suffering or hardship. We come through these times with a stronger sense of faith and look back on our experiences, wondering how we survived. Survival is faith, and we need to trust in ourselves.

A sense of faith will eventually lead us to surrender our problems more easily, knowing that we are always looked after and that the problems and difficulties we face are, without question, for our own benevolence.

God wants us to rediscover God, but how. Man has created a great many problems for himself and I feel God is using these problems to recreate faith, which is faith in God. The faith in God will be re-established as man falters in confusion and desperation, finally realising that he has run dry of intellectual answers and scientific hogwash. We drive ourselves to the very edge of the abyss, and just as we are in danger of falling, God stoops down and lifts us into The Arms of Divinity.

Real faith is not gained through a church or instructor but comes from within. You know that you have faith when you are at ease and completely satisfied with yourself. A person who is at peace with himself is at one with God. Faith is an innate quality of goodness, wisdom and purity. Faith is knowing yourself, being one with your Spirit, understanding the existence of God within yourself and in every human being. Faith is realised, not learnt, it is the internal manifestation of holiness.

If we only had faith in ourselves, then we would have faith in God, and once again, learn to respect nature and all the animals, trees and plants that live within it. Once that faith is established within ourselves, we have inner confidence and the total power of our own convictions.

Chapter 7

Self Respect

Wednesday 13th July 1994, Playa de los Genoveses, Beach in the Natural Park near San José, Almeria, Spain

The following day, Abi and I decided to take a drive to a beach that had been recommended to us. This beach had been described as one of the most beautiful beaches in Southern Spain, and it lived up to its promise, a bay surrounded by sand dunes and palm trees, with mountains on either side. It was the end of the day when we arrived and families were packing up their belongings and heading for home. It wasn't long before Abi and I were left alone in this idyllic location.

The sun was setting and a strong wind was blowing in from the sea. Large waves were breaking on the beach. I looked across the beach towards the mountain and it turned into Shri Ganesha, three hundred feet tall. Shri Ganesha danced across the beach in front of us, in Shri Ganesha's own unique style, which had become so familiar to me. Then suddenly Shri Ganesha was gone. I looked back towards the mountain, and slowly Shri Ganesha's Elephant Head appeared from behind it, Shri Ganesha smiled in a wonderful, childlike, playful way.

Out of the sea came Angels and Deities, and I ran to greet Them. By the time I arrived at the sea's edge, They had disappeared. I slowly strolled down the beach, thinking how incredibly playful and imaginative Divinity was. I reached the end of the beach and decided to run back through the water. I could taste the salt in my mouth from the spray.

In the middle of the bay, at the water's edge, I felt the power of the wind and the waves. I closed my eyes and bowed my head in respect to the sea. Slowly raising my head and opening my eyes, I saw that the whole scene in front of me had changed. I was suddenly looking into The Mouth of The Great Mother. The sea was inside Mother's Mouth, and Mother's Head filled the sky.

I felt joy welling up inside me as I tore my clothes off and dived into the sea, into God's Mouth.

As I swim,
I feel the warmth of the sea –
Mother's Saliva.
I feel the warm wind
The spray of the waves breaking over my head.
At this moment,
Mother is Everything.
The whole sea is Divinity,
I am inside The Body of my Mother.
The Earth is God
Mother Earth is a living being.

This newly awakened sense of respect for the Earth reminded me of my childhood, when I felt a similar feeling of respect for my grandfather. I saw myself sitting on his knee at the table after lunch, feeling that same sense of dignity and love – the way he would slowly peel an apple with his penknife. I could innately feel his patience and respect and love for life, and I wanted to learn the essence of life from him.

How can we learn to treat each other with more respect and humility. In order to respect one another, we must first have respect for ourselves. Self-respect comes from the ability to look after yourself. Respecting your body, mind and Spirit. Treating yourself with love and patience. All of this comes from an unconscious respect for God.

Later that evening, we visited a little fishing village for dinner. As I was sitting there, I could feel the collective warmth of Spanish family life. The children were still up at ten o'clock, playing. People walking, babies, parents, grandparents, all together enjoying as one.

I can see God in all the children, spontaneous, natural, joyful, playful, and beautiful – the jewels of our society.

I looked up and the moon was shining across the sea, the sky was clear, the stars were twinkling – and then the moon turned into Mother's Face as Mother smiled down on us.

Chapter 8

Truth

Thursday 14th July 1994, 4pm
I know the time has come for even greater revelations. It is strange to feel The Truth so clearly and directly and yet, moments later, to feel so humble, in meditation. So utterly thoughtless and peaceful. At one with myself.

In this state, it is as if I have turned into love. I cannot feel anything but love. The connection is changing. New feelings are emerging that I am finding difficult to express.

The Truth is incredibly penetrating. I can see now that by using The Truth in the right way, one can penetrate people's hearts, to move, motivate and liberate them, to lift them higher and encompass them in love. Direct Truth is nothing but Absolute Love because Pure Knowledge and Pure Truth are vibrations emanating from The Divine.

Truth is Love and Love is Truth, you cannot change or compromise it, you just eventually become it.

I thank You, Mother, from my heart.
I never knew The Truth could be so powerful,
Beyond all our beliefs and dreams.
Herald The Golden Age!
The time has come to express God's Love.
That which is done from the heart,
Can change the world.

The heart breathes,
Emitting goodness and love.

Through a desire to please, by sincerely wanting to help one another, our hearts will naturally open and our way of life will change. We don't even need to ask how this will happen. Perhaps if we know in our hearts that something is going to happen, by simply opening our hearts, then it will happen. Through your own heart, you will awaken and enlighten other people's hearts.

Sometimes the answers are so obvious that we cannot see them.

Fear has crept into our society and has become the disease of modern life. We fear the very act of loving and caring. Once our heart is closed, fear comes through our ego because we cannot accept love. Our denial of love only adds to our fear. Nowadays we cannot even open the door without asking who is there.

Where does all this fear come from. Perhaps it comes from a lack of motherhood. Without love and nourishment in our family life, our children become fearful. Something that should be so natural – the love between a mother and a child – has for some reason become difficult and problematic. Without that nurturing feminine quality, everything is destroyed.

One of the most beautiful images of western culture is the Virgin Mother with baby Jesus. That image has the capacity to invoke such a feeling of love and compassion and responsibility. Our children are God's children. We must love and cherish them, so they can grow in a stable environment with open hearts, and no fear to break this cycle. With open hearts, all of that fear would be eradicated and once again, our lives would be full of warmth and understanding.

Self-knowledge comes from a sense of humility. If we are humble, then it is easier to love and if we love, everything works out. But how do we bring this about. How do we emancipate the world. By desiring together that we change. By prayer, by faith, by God, Who is always there to help us, even though we deny God. We pretend that God doesn't exist, but God does. God wants to help us, all it depends upon, is our own desire.

I pray with my whole heart that people will feel this love and will benefit from it.

I surrender to The Will of God, The Power of the Cosmos.

Chapter 9

River Of Life

Thursday 14th July 1994

Sitting on the terrace of our small stone cottage, enjoying the warmth of the sun and the fresh mountain air, I remembered that we had been asked to water the crops in front of the house.

I had spent the last few days looking at the plants and the trees, thinking to myself how clever the farmers are here, that they design the growth of their crops on a slope, so that all you need to do is to put a hose in one position and the water would run all the way round the crops in little trenches and would even go to the individual trees.

I got the hose. Placing it where I thought was the right position, I waited for the water to run off down the trenches, but in fact the water ran to my feet. So I moved the hose and the water still ran towards me. I suddenly realised that Mother Earth had produced a Maya, an illusion. I had believed the lay of the land to be one way, when in fact it wasn't, it was sloping in the opposite direction. I moved the hose again, to the other end, and it slowly trickled round the crops.

Sometimes in life we think we know The Truth, and that Truth is something we can understand and possess, but perhaps we should look again. Truth is what it is. The water cannot run uphill. We may have to open our minds and hearts in order to understand Truth, because it may not be what we thought it was.

It is amazing how many lessons can be learnt from simply watering the garden. By watering the plants, I found The Truth, which was in the lay of the land. If I hadn't picked up the hose and tested it, I would still be living in that illusion. So, it is important in life, if someone expresses what he claims to be The Truth, to try it for ourselves and to test it. If it's right, we will know.

I was really enjoying watering the crops and trees and I was trying to work out, 'what is this enjoyment.' What was it within me that was enjoying watering the plants. Well, it was a feeling of love, to be part of the process of natural growth. I could feel that the water coming from the hose was pure love, because it gave life and nourishment. If the water is love, then the trees and plants and fruits become love. If the fruits are love, and we eat the fruit, we too become love.

Love is so incredibly simple, it can be water, soil or sand... it is all God. God and Love are one thing. God is all around us, everywhere. All we have to do is realise it and feel it. Once that happens to us, everything changes.

When a mother has a baby, we want to nourish the baby, by giving it water and food. That nourishment is love. We have to become like the water and food, to nourish one another, so that we may grow, like the plants I was watering that morning. And when we are asked to do something, we can try and feel a sense of love in any task we carry out. Then we will feel love in our hearts because we are giving and pleasing one another.

I am suddenly able to understand how the earth is made of many different elements, and how we are made in exactly the same proportions of elements – which means that if we are the same, and the earth is love, then we too can become love, and everything will be solved.

It is as if the discovery of life has come from Mother Earth Herself, that is where we began and where we will return. In between is confusion, but we will overcome it.

While watering the garden, I could see that by drawing analogies between man and the elements, we could more readily understand life and love, because we already feel empathy towards the awesome greatness of Mother Earth.

Rain. It rains because the whole ecological system wants to survive. The earth creates rain to give back life to itself. When rain falls on a mountain, the mountain doesn't say, I want to keep all this water for myself. He takes what he needs and lets the rest flow down to the valleys and the lowlands, where we can grow crops to retain life on Earth. That is how the mountain and the rain give love to the valleys and to us.

We can learn from Mother Earth and realise that if we want to help one another in society, we must give love and nourishment, unconditionally. After all, the mountain makes no conditions on the valleys. We have to learn that real love is unconditional. If we expect anything back in payment, then it is not real love. It becomes warped and unnourishable. Like the wise mountain that lets go of the water, we need to understand that love is something that cannot be imposed upon another person. It is something to be shared.

In the world today, we benefit from such enormous wealth. We could use this wealth unconditionally, to help others in a positive way – not expecting anything in return, which only increases and pampers our ego. The more we give, the more we will get back in return. We are made in the reflection of God and we can learn from the earth. Just as God loves Himself, we too can learn to love ourselves and grow in our sense of self-respect.

If the mountains were to keep the rain and the valleys had no water, then all life would die. Likewise, if we want to hurt ourselves, we can. And we do. We die from terrible diseases, which need not affect us if we use the power of love, the nourishment of all beings. With that sense of love, we will nourish our own growth and eradicate all diseases known to man. But if we are selfish and uncompromising with our love, we will punish ourselves and finally perish.

The power of love is enormous. We have not yet tapped into the tremendous healing powers of love. Mother Nature is being damaged by man, yet Mother Nature still loves us, still nourishes us and cares for us. But every so often Mother Nature gives us a warning, just to let us know who is boss.

I am convinced that we will eventually become knowledge, love and wisdom, and end up knowing and understanding everything that there is to know. Perhaps what we need to do is to concentrate upon the qualities of life, compassion and love, instead of seeing the negative side of people.

If someone is aggressive, we don't need to put our attention on the aggression. We can direct our attention to God in their heart. God in their heart is Love in their heart. Everybody has it, we just need to find it. Once we have found it within them, they will smile. Once they have smiled, we have opened up another channel for God's Love.

I feel that our growth will come from The Love of God. After all, God loves His children. Mother loves us all. Mother is our Protector, our Comforter, our Redeemer and The Saviour of mankind.

I must once again trust in my own convictions – and be convinced of them.

As I sat at the table on the terrace, Mother asked me, "How much proof do you need. Are you still looking for gratitude. Are you looking for praise."

Mother said, "Truth is what it is, there is no praise."

Chapter 10

Forgiveness

Saturday 16th July 1994, 9pm
(Dictaphone)
It was Saturday evening, and we were having dinner outside a restaurant in a small village up in the mountains. For the first time in weeks, I was feeling hot and irritable, and had a slight headache. At the same time, I could also feel a sense of oppression, almost like a blanket over Spain. It felt as if their whole society was suffering, perhaps from previous karmas and deeds. There seemed to be an underlying unhappiness within the people and sometimes when we had gone for breakfast at eight or nine in the morning, the men would be drinking large brandies and already be drunk. In my new-found state of Awareness, I felt sick in their presence.

I could feel that Shri Ganesha, The Aspect of Innocence and Wisdom, had not yet awakened or manifested in this society. Lord Jesus Christ is an Incarnation of Shri Ganesha, so I prayed to Lord Jesus to forgive them, and asked Mother to lift off the blanket, to eradicate the ignorance.

There was something strange about the behaviour of the children playing around us in this village. They were fighting and being irritable with one another, and this was making me uncomfortable. I prayed to Mother to awaken The Powers of Shri Ganesha.

I could suddenly feel a cool soothing breeze. The atmosphere was changing. Our hearts began to open and the heaviness was dispelled. Mother appeared and sat in a chair beside me. Mother pushed Mother's Thumb onto my forehead, I could feel myself being soothed and nourished with Divine Love.

What is incredible about these experiences is that God is an actualisation. This is not a blind faith, but total connection to God.

Mother is sitting here, completely in meditation, and I am wondering what Mother is meditating upon. Suddenly it feels as if the whole of Spain has awakened and turned into The Innocence of Shri Ganesha. The whole place feels alive. The mountains around us have turned into thousands of Shri Ganeshas and Mother is smiling at us. I cannot believe it. There is now a strong cool breeze blowing. My heart and head have cleared completely and my anger has vanished.

Later that same evening, I knew it was time to move on. We decided to go back to the cottage, pack up all our belongings and head for Malaga, a four-hour drive away. We agreed to do this in absolute silence, and then just drive through the night. I paid the bill, and we drove back to the cottage along the winding mountain road.

In complete silence, we cleaned the cottage, gathered our things and were soon heading to Malaga. After an hour, Abi fell asleep. I could feel Mother sitting in the car with us, behind me, enjoying the journey. The Divine loves spontaneity and this certainly felt like a spontaneous journey.

I'd grown to enjoy this part of the night, from midnight to dawn. As we neared Malaga, I wondered where we would be staying, and suddenly I could see Mother opening a hotel bedroom door. I peered into the room which was soft but at the same time formal, with sliding doors onto a balcony overlooking the port. I could also see a swimming pool. I felt I had to get to Malaga to find this hotel.

Chapter 11

Love Yourself

Saturday 16th and Monday 18th July 1994, Malaga

We arrived in central Malaga at about 3.30 a.m. It was elevating and uplifting to be connected to so many human beings again. As we drove through the old city, people were spilling out of the night clubs and bars, and I could feel the youth of Spain, beautiful young people in the prime of their lives. I could feel all of their hearts and God within them. I just let the car take us where it wanted to go.

We ended up at about five in the morning at a small bed and breakfast. A lady came to the door in her nightgown and didn't seem bothered by the time.

When we woke up later that morning, we decided to go in search of the hotel that Mother had shown me in my vision. We visited a few hotels but they just didn't seem right. As we came out of one of these places, I looked across the road to see an enormous hotel that looked as if it could be the right one. We walked over and entered the foyer. The hotel had a big marbled entrance hall, and it felt Divine, absolutely cool and soothing. This seemed to be the one. We asked to see a room and were taken up to the eleventh floor.

The porter opened the door and I knew immediately this was the same room. I walked onto the balcony, and sure enough, the view was over the port. But there was obviously no swimming pool as the hotel was right in the centre of town. We decided to stay. I could feel The Divine with us and that our path and journey had been chosen. We spent the day walking around the old part of Malaga, enjoying the Spanish way of life and the architecture of this ancient city. Later on, back at the hotel, I fell asleep for my usual late afternoon nap.

I wake up. Mother is sitting on a chair in the room. Mother looks beautiful and is changing from being a young girl into a mother and then into a grandmother and back again. I bow down before Mother and then sit at Mother's Feet. I feel that I am becoming an instrument of God.

Mother is God, and Mother tells me that if I can love myself, then I am Mother, I am Mother.

I reply, How can I be a part of You and accept You.

"Love yourself."

What does that mean.

"God is Love", Mother tells me, "So, if you love yourself then you are part of God. But you have to sincerely love yourself and know that you love yourself, and wholeheartedly understand that you love yourself".

At that moment, God is everywhere. In every room, in every city, in every space, everywhere.

I have never felt God so strongly as right now.
I surrender to The Power of The Divine,
To The Will of God.
I feel The Virgin Mother in my hands,
As The Holy Ghost,
And I feel the power of realisation.

Abi burst into the room to inform me that there was a big procession going on outside and that people were taking a statue of The Virgin Mary out on their boats to parade around the port.

The Great Mother is now towering over Malaga with Mother's Back to the procession. Mother is pouring light into the old part of the city. I desire that the people in the procession would feel The Divinity around them. Suddenly, The Great Mother turns to face them and begins working on them, pouring vibrations into them. I wish that it was this Real Living Mother on their boat and not a statue of The Virgin Mary.

I can feel a heaviness coming from the people, as if all of their problems and conditionings are being drawn out of them. A feeling of oppression and darkness starts to come towards the hotel. On every balcony and on the roof of this huge hotel, I can see Angels, Gods and Goddesses with weapons for the destruction of this black mass of negativity.

Suddenly, out through the top of my head comes an enormous Angel with a huge sword, leading all The Divine Beings into battle. While Mother looks on with love, this Divine Army slashes, destroys and annihilates the black mass of negativity that was emanating from the procession.

I now feel joy in all the hearts of the people - something has happened.

Back in the room, Mother is seated before me and there are tears in Mother's Eyes.

Every tear is like an ocean of forgiveness,
Like an awesome petal from Mother's Heart.
All I can think is that I love Mother more than ever.
May The Will of God be in everyone's heart,
And the emancipation of mankind be on the march.
Things are going to change,
I feel it in my heart.

Mother is now telling us to get ready, to go out and enjoy ourselves, to spread the vibrations, to open our hearts to all the people and to enjoy. I want to say much more but cannot find the words. I could speak all night, forever, about The Beauty and about The Wholeness and The Tremendous Power of God. I am on a wave of Divine Vibrations. It's like Jerusalem is being built at this moment.

I don't know if I have the authority,
But on behalf of every human being,
I pray to The Mother
And to God Almighty
To Help us.

Later that same evening, there is something very primordial about the whole lounge area of the hotel. Every chair is occupied by a God or Deity of some description, as if in Heaven. I seem to be holding the world in my hands and my head feels as if it is opening out. An Angel appears out of me, and stands behind me, protectively.

Mother arrives. Everyone stands to clap and to sing a Divine Song. The whole ceiling is filled with Mother's Face and now Mother is sitting in front of me in many different forms. Mother is young, full of joy and innocence. Suddenly Mother turns into The Primordial Mother, awesomely powerful.

I want to ask Mother to help me not to have any doubts and not to worry about what I see and feel. To help me to accept it. I want to accept it but I still keep worrying and doubting and thinking that people won't understand. Mother is shaking Mother's Finger at me, telling me not to doubt. To have no doubts. Mother is young again. Angels are surrounding Mother. Mother says that Mother could see doubt in my face and says to me, “Take it away, don’t doubt any more” – and it’s gone.

I ask Mother now to take me deeper, for more Divine Inspiration. I feel as if Heaven is opening before me and I am bowing at Mother’s Feet. I just want to feel simple and humble. I’d like Mother to take me deeper into this beautiful World. Mother asks me if I’m ready. I am. Mother, please strengthen my belief, my faith and my love for You. I can now feel Mother’s Love welling within me. My face is changing, I no longer feel human. I am drinking from The Ocean of Nectar and that beyond all doubt is Jerusalem, The Golden City.

The experience is growing, getting stronger and stronger. My heart opens and I can see the Universe within it. It feels as if the room has disappeared. There is only Heaven. I ask The Mother to destroy any fear within me. This is a primordial event, above every aspect of human awareness.

This is The Reality of Doubtless Awareness.

Mother is asking me to fly with Mother. I am travelling around the Universe with Mother and have gone beyond all desires and normal awareness, into completely new perceptions. My senses are very different and once again I ask to go deeper.

Now I feel I am actually inside Mother, going into Mother’s Soul. Mother says, “Trust me.” Never before have I had a journey like this. It seems that I have left my body. Suddenly to my surprise, I am also part of the earth, and I am travelling at a very great speed towards the centre of it. I want to stay in this state forever. My whole body is cleansed, my organs and spiritual centres are spinning, I have no ego or superego and I am weightless, in a new time, space and energy.

I can see myself dancing around the room with The Various Deities. My senses are heightened, as if I could hear a pin drop in France. I desire to be in Mother's Heart. Mother's Heart opens and I step into it. Suddenly I feel Divinity inside me with a force I have never experienced before. I am warm and soothed and at the same time I feel as if there is a fountain of Divine Vibrations coming out of my head. I am expanding and changing and I surrender in totality. I give up everything.

I would like to stay in this state forever. I have no more doubts, how could I ever have had any doubts. I recognise that we are all just children, lost. All we really want to do is be in our Mother's Arms, to feel The Love of Divinity and to go beyond all of our human problems and conditionings.

The porter comes into the lounge and is wandering from table to table, switching off the lights. He turns out the light by our table and we are plunged into darkness, as if we are not there.

The next morning, I awoke from a beautiful sleep and we decided after breakfast to find the beach in Malaga. We spent a very enjoyable day watching the Spanish children playing in the water, and after lunch, we decided to go back to the hotel. As we got closer to the hotel, I could see Mother standing on the roof, very still, silent. I wondered why Mother was actually on the roof, was it to show us where the hotel was.

Back in the room, Abi decided she wanted to sit on a sunny balcony and so rang the reception to ask them if she could use another balcony. The receptionist replied, Why don't you use our lovely pool on the roof. Abi screamed with joy and told me that there was a swimming pool on the roof after all. We both grabbed our towels and arrived on the roof of the hotel to find the most beautiful swimming pool with sunshades and lovely wicker chairs, with no one there but Mother and us.

We dived into the pool and realised that Mother does know everything.

Chapter 12

Reality

19th July 1994, Malaga, Spain, Malaga Palace Hotel Lounge, midnight

(Dictaphone)

That evening, as we are sitting in the hotel lounge, I go into meditation.

Mother is sitting on the sofa in front of me and to Mother's left is William Blake, dressed in the period costume of that time. I ask William Blake whether He feels His work had been fulfilled. William Blake looks as if He cannot express Himself, as if He was somehow prevented from being able to describe The Glory of God and our Mother.

Shri Krishna arrives, wearing beautiful sandals and a dhoti, with many jewels and a crown on His head. Shri Krishna sits down, and here we are once again in this Heavenly place. These Deities, Incarnations and Aspects of God, are each of a very individual character, because They represent different times in our evolution and also different aspects and qualities within every human being. It is quite amazing to be here with Them.

Now, for some reason, I begin to doubt that this is happening. Abi and I start to argue, and Shri Krishna, The Lord of Diplomacy, attempts to calm us. Mother is in complete meditation and so is William Blake. They are ignoring us, and now Shri Krishna has also gone into meditation. Abi and I realise how foolish it is to argue and how human it is. I realise in this state that we must be very careful and auspicious in order to understand and observe The Protocol of God. I bow to God Almighty, to Mother and to all The Deities and pray for Them to help us.

The Divine Mother turns slowly into The Virgin Mary and now Mother is enormous, towering over Malaga. Mother bows to the city. I feel strong waves of realisation and of awakenings within myself, which seem to connect me to Universal Love through the top of my head. Waves of cool vibrations, soothing every pore of my body, and a strong connection with The Mother Earth.

Once again there is a sense of Divinity rejoicing. Angels are assembling. The ceiling opens and there are Angels above.

My senses are heightened and I can feel the mood and vibrations of Malaga. It seems that The Divine Mother has turned into The Virgin Mary because the Spanish respect the qualities of The Mother within their society, and because of the large part played by The Virgin Mary in their religion. Those beautiful qualities of femininity, of motherhood and of nourishment, have to be respected and loved. I pray to The Divine Mother to help us feel those qualities and to help us recognise God within ourselves.

This morning, when I was wandering around the city, all the old people seemed to be trapped and entrenched into their catholicism. Their bodies looked old and twisted, not able to really accept or understand The Truth. But I could feel the vibrations of the younger people, that The Power of God was awakened in them and that they could see the failings of catholicism. I pray that The Truth will prevail, that the old conditionings will be destroyed and that a wonderful New World will be created.

I ask Mother to take me into a deeper state of meditation and as I ask, I feel the vibrations increasing immensely. Abi asks me a question, Which is reality. This world, or the state that you are now in. The Divine Mother answers the question by laughing and then smiling towards me. Mother does not say anything, but that is the answer.

This New World of Divinity is the most powerful Reality – so enlightening and enriched with beauty and wonder. I keep asking Mother to take me further into Heaven and realise that Mother has brought it here. It's all around us. I pray to Mother to bring all The Angels and all The Deities to this place so that we can worship Them all in our hearts, and now I feel there is a celebration happening.

This Reality is The Truth and Truth is Reality. There is no greater truth than God and there is no reality greater than God. I feel that the whole point of this new-found Awareness and Consciousness is to experience and establish Heaven on Earth and to rejoice in the unveiling of God in a way never thought possible before.

The world we have created is an illusion, created through our ego and intellect, which is now rendering us blind to The Truth. We have hidden The Truth in a maze, and we have built so many backwaters, so many dead ends within our own minds and consciousness, that we have completely destroyed our connection with God. Somehow this needs to be unravelled, to be opened out to a path of Truth.

Perhaps it will help to share these experiences, so that we can realise that there is much beyond our understanding of God. Somehow, we have to surrender, we have to be humble and know that we don't have all the answers. God will hear our prayers and then The Truth will shine forth in an everlasting eternity of goldenness.

I now feel like I don't exist at all. I just hear a voice, there is no body and I am only The Spirit. My eyes are closed and I have gone deeper tonight. I am aware of Angels all around me. I am being inspired to new heights of Divine Perception and Reality.

Everything in this state is nurtured and looked after. There is love, and everything a person could ever want or desire is right here now in this room, in this Consciousness. What we have created for ourselves is very little, but there is an enormous potential within all of us. It only needs to be awakened and from there our enlightenment will rise up. Then we will be able to forgive one another and we will be able to see a new transformation emerging within humanity.

I humbly request for help, and The Divine Mother presses Mother's Left Hand into my forehead. Any pain remaining within me is melted away, and my head feels as light as a feather. This feeling of lightness and of tranquillity is beautifully Divine.

In this state, I see that if we could understand and accept God, then we could work out our problems together and live in Reality with all the good things that we have created.

Having this realisation, I completely adore this Mother Aspect of God. With my whole heart, I only want to be in Your Arms and to sleep there for eternity.

Suddenly, the whole roof of the hotel has been blown off and we are accelerating upwards into Heaven. Now we have gone into Heaven. I can't see, I can't feel. I don't really know what is happening. I ask for more love and more compassion in my heart and in my head. Now I feel as if I am being split in half by this beautiful Power within me. I pray that everyone will experience this. I don't want it just for myself, I want everyone to have it and I open my heart and ask God to give it to as many people as possible.

Real love and real compassion is detachment. We catch on our hearts because we are too attached to our human needs and worries. The Divine is holding out all the answers, all we need to do is to go that bit further and deeper and we will be given all the answers.

All of a sudden, I feel home and London coming into my attention. We all choose our place of birth, so I must have chosen London, The Heart of God. Such a wonderful place. I pray to Lord Shiva, The Deity of England, to open the hearts of the English people and to rid us of our obsession with materialism. I am sure that if we could drop this obsession, we would then have everything we need. It's like we are chasing our tails, running around and around and getting absolutely nowhere. All we need to do is take one step back and one step upwards towards God. Our evolution and problems would be solved. The nut of the heart would finally be broken, and now it feels like this is beginning to happen.

I feel like singing and dancing and laughing because that is what inspires me.

Alcoholism is also crushing us, putting pressure on us and closing the heart by creating heat and anger within us. I can see multitudes of power intoxicated men with red faces, barking at one another, arguing over their beer and going home having not answered any questions, and waking up the next day feeling awful. I ask God to put Divine Vibrations into the alcohol so that it has no effect any more.

The Great Mother is telling me the reason why the Western world is going through so many pains and problems. Believe it or not, these hardships are caused by the alcohol and drugs in our society. We are spending so much money on them. It's such a waste, and if we could stop these nonsensical things, then we would become wealthy overnight. Just like smoking, alcohol will go out of evolution.

It has to, because it is impure. The way forward is through surrender and joy and there are all the answers in this Ocean of Divine Consciousness.

If only we could open our eyes to see our imperfections, introspect and change what we have created, look into the mirror and find the faults and cracks and mend them, we would then grow strong like warriors.

Chapter 13

It's Up To You

20th July 1994, Malaga Airport, midday
(Dictaphone)
It is time to return to England. We pack up our bags and head for Malaga Airport. When we arrive there, we can feel all the tension of the people as they rush around madly trying to get their planes on time, as if it would be the end of the world if they were to miss their flight. But we are very quiet, in meditation, sitting at a table in the airport just watching and witnessing all the people.

I feel Divinity in this place. It is such a blessing to be getting to know The Divine. We are really so lucky to have this gift of Realisation. I begin to realise that I am taking it for granted, wandering around with everything working out in front of me. It's wonderful to be in this Reality, in a kind of dream, and to know that it is not a dream, that it is true.

There is no confusion, stress or strain, just The Divine Flow of Life.

Divinity is timeless, so we don't have to worry much about the plane. A few of God's Names spring to mind. Faultless Brilliance, that God is awakened in Mother's devotees, unnoticed by others, like the Swan on the Manasa Lake. That seems to be the trick, to be awakened and to remain humble, so nobody is aware. It has its own disguise, hidden, quietly waiting for the right moment. There are so many beautiful people in the world, with tremendous love and qualities within them. I can only think of Blake's Words at this moment, as I sit back relaxing, drinking a glass of Coca-Cola. I change Blake's Words into a modern-day theme, 'to see the Universe in a glass of Coca-Cola and infinity in an airport lounge'.

In spite of all this realisation, I am having to come to terms with my own problems and inadequacies. We all know that we are really seeking Ultimate Love and satisfaction, but when I think of my life in particular, and the problems I have had with relationships, it is starting to become clearer.

In our so-called love relationships, we 'fall in love' with someone, but what this really means is that we have become infatuated or fascinated by a person's outward image. It is not necessarily a spiritual love. For the first few months, in this type of relationship, we both give lots of love, happiness and joy. Then after a while, it becomes clear that the relationship has no real firm basis, and we move on to the next liaison. So, this cycle of unhappiness and searching for love, carries on unrewarded. All we do is hurt ourselves. What a nightmare. No wonder we are all in a mess.

If love were unconditional then it would flow, like nature. Our hearts would open and the love would be pure. When I meditate, I can feel unconditional love flowing through me. But at the same time, I see all the conditionings I've developed over the last thirty-seven years, which create an obstacle to this natural flow. Hopefully, we will one day be rid of all our bad conditionings and our journey into God's Arms will be completed.

I pray to our Divine Mother to be here with me always, and suddenly I feel that Mother is returning the compliment by saying, "It's up to you". It's so obvious really, if we want something so pure, we have to desire it with all our heart.

When what we have craved and desired for the whole of our existence is suddenly before us, all we can do is falter. But the faltering is also helping us to see and realise the problems and conditions we have created. Through our ability to see for the first time through the eyes of our own Spirit, we can eradicate these conditionings and finally become our true self.

Divinity is soothing and calming, but at the same time, enormously dynamic. God can be awakened in somebody like that, in a second. Divinity never stays still, it is always moving, working and growing. It knows the optimum time to be in any one place, and then moves on. Like flowers, always growing yet we can't see them grow.

Man has to achieve his Realisation, which is The Awakening of God within him. Once God is awakened, then our desire, attention and awareness changes. We become collectively conscious and interested in the collective growth of mankind. I have become aware that God can only work through human desire, and that God and mankind have to work together in harmony. God wants man to evolve, but in order to evolve, we need to reach The Divinity within us.

I surrender to The Divine Mother and ask Mother for inspiration on the journey home. Now, on the plane, as we start to taxi down the runway, once again I can feel the tension in all the people. But I feel completely relaxed and unperturbed as the plane hurtles down the runway towards take-off.

The Divine Mother is sitting with me, in meditation, completely unaffected by the tensions and concerns of all the people, as if in an armchair at home. Not an ounce of tension or fear, just sweet Consciousness. I too relax and try to see if I can have no reactions. Divinity is pouring from this Divine

Personality – so relaxed, so harmonious and so spontaneous, it is simply unbelievable.

One minute spent in this Consciousness with The Primordial Divine Mother is worth lifetimes. I can feel in this Consciousness that there is no guilt, and that the guilt within us is very destructive. We punish ourselves and are saying sorry all the time. If only we could eradicate this guilt, then we would all become our true selves, much easier going, more accepting and understanding.

Guilt also leads us in some ways to become intellectual. I don't think that I have ever been intellectual, and I'm not sure I could be. I don't understand this modernism, this twentieth century wisdom, by which you think you know everything when you know absolutely nothing. Once you start intellectualising, you miss the point of Truth and Reality because you are trying to rationalise The Truth, which is beyond the mind.

I see now how the human mind analyses and judges everything. We have destroyed our Pure and Natural Art by criticising one another to the point where we cannot perform for fear of criticism. But Pure Art is God – nothing more, nothing less. Visions of God, a connection with God. It has always been said that nations should follow art, because following art is following God, so long as it is Pure Art.

I always wondered how to discriminate between good and bad art, but Real Art is born of God. Mozart, Blake, Michelangelo, C.S. Lewis – these are real artists, the realised souls who could see and follow The Truth and Art in God. Simple and wonderful. God can work through people in so many incredible ways.

We've now landed at Manchester Airport and guess what. Can I remember where we parked the car in the long-term car park. There is no need to worry though. If we don't find the car today, we'll probably find it tomorrow. Time is only a creation of man, so I am sure that if we surrender, then we will find it.

Chapter 14

The Home Coming

22nd July and 1st August 1994

I went to visit a friend of mine who I hadn't seen for a while. He is probably my closest friend and we have always had a very strong bond of understanding between us.

I described my recent experiences to him, how The Feminine Aspect of God would manifest to me. He asked me if we could experience it now, here, at his flat. We had some tea together and afterwards we sat on the floor in front of his sofa.

We both go into meditation, and it is not long before The Divine Mother is sitting on the sofa, also in deep meditation. Mother suddenly looks straight at us, smiling, as if pleased to be here.

I feel my head opening, and now Mother is standing over London. It is quite amazing how, in this state, I can distinctly feel the different vibrations of London. Here in South London the vibrations are very different to Central London, rather more heavy. Mother is pouring light into the whole area. Mother's Attention, along with our own attention, has gone into all the houses in London and on to everyone's heart.

Now the ceiling is opening up and there are Angels everywhere. One of Them is standing right in front of me, The One I now call The Protecting Angel. It feels as though we may be about to go on some kind of mission. The Angels are talking to The Great Mother and the room has somehow increased in volume. Normally only about fifteen square feet, the room now seems enormous, as if we have gone beyond our normal rational time and space, and it is filled with incredibly powerful Deities and Angels.

At the same time, Mother is asking us to forgive and to clear our minds. The vibrations here are still quite blocked and heavy. Mother is asking us to be joyous, not to be serious, to open our hearts. Mother is banging Mother's Foot and hitting Mother's Knees and laughing very joyously, and now I feel that Mother is manifesting out of our hearts and Mother seems very pleased.

All of a sudden, we are five hundred feet above the flat, looking down into the room, but at the same time sitting at The Feet of our Divine Mother. Mother asks us to feel God in everyone's heart in the whole of London. I suddenly see London as a heart, as The Heart of Lord Shiva. Our hearts and minds are so connected, and once again Mother is asking us to forgive and to open our minds. Mother has put Mother's Hand on my forehead. My entire head is melting and being soothed. I ask Mother if there is anything to desire to help clear London and Mother says, "Yes", that we need to go into deeper meditation.

Suddenly, I feel rose petals falling all around us, like gifts from Heaven, rejoicing in our recognition. I can feel The Beauty of God, the amazing inspiration and subtlety. Mother is asking us not to be tense, or heavy. We carry so much tension as human beings, and our ego always feels heavy. We've all cried so much in the wilderness, we've all cried so much at night. Cried to feed on the answers of pain. Cried to find a piece of Truth. One piece of Truth to see us through to the morning. Now Mother is whacking me on the head, which feels incredible, absolutely amazing.

The Divine Vibrations are really increasing now, and Mother is saying that as English people, we should try to laugh and enjoy ourselves more. Mother also acknowledges my friend, which is wonderful, as Mother has not done so before this moment.

Mother has never been so clear before. Normally, Mother is in meditation, but now Mother is extremely vivid and is staring at us very intently. A Deity has emerged from my friend and is dancing around us. It seems that we no longer exist as human beings, that we have gone beyond, that we no longer have bodies and that we exist now only in a spiritual form.

We have taken off, holding hands, and are going on a trip around London. We are sprinkling rose petals all around London for the people to walk upon. I ask The Divine Mother to take us deeper into meditation. Now Mother is sitting upright with a crown on Mother's Head, looking very much younger.

Another battle is taking place, as if God is calling in the troops. Angels are appearing from every direction. At the same time, I can feel the strong qualities of England being awakened. I pray that the qualities of The Heart will manifest in the people of our society and that they will recognise God within themselves. A tremendous depth of heart and goodness will definitely come forth in our society. I pray to The Divine Mother that The Heart will rejoice, will manifest and give praise to God. I desire the destruction of all the negativity in London.

Now I feel the manifestation of Shri Ganesha, The Lord of Wisdom and Innocence, who is dancing around The Great Mother while The Angels rejoice.

Our hearts have turned into flowers. The wild daisies of England. This is Reality, The Pure Reality of Thoughtless

Awareness, being in the present, here and now. When we are in the present, we are in the presence of God, Who is within us and all around us.

Angels appear on every street corner, handing out flowers to everyone and asking them to place them on their hearts. Mother tells us to have faith, in ourselves and everyone else, and that it requires tremendous faith to feel and to be with God.

A connection exists between our heart and our faith because faith comes from the heart, directly from God Almighty. Our heart is The Spirit and The Reflection of God.

Now, very significantly, all The Angels are singing 'Jerusalem'. Our egos are being dissolved and our hearts have grown out of all proportion within us. We are turning into Shri Ganesha. Once your heart is open and your ego has melted away, you turn into a child and manifest as innocence. The world has turned into Heaven on Earth. My arms feel like those of Shri Ganesha, my head has turned into Shri Ganesha's and I have Shri Ganesha's Ears.

God has all the answers to everything, for God is Shri Ganesha and we are all God's children. Now there is no ego, there is nothing. The history of man is really quite simple. We have gained our ego through our free will, but now we can lose our ego, become the heart and regain the innocence of a child. Then we will have completed our journey back into our Mother's Arms.

I have now turned completely into innocence. I bow to God and thank God from my heart. With a sense of awe, I realise that this takes me back to a recurring dream of my childhood. I would wake up and think, 'What is this state'. It was the most indescribable feeling, and now I am experiencing it again, racing back through time at a million miles an hour and I could stay in this state forever.

I understand something I have never understood before, that evil and wicked people try to destroy the good ones, try to destroy their innocence. It takes tremendous strength to overcome these attacks in our life, but somehow God guides us on our journey. It is a tremendous journey to find God, and once we have found God, we must never let go. We will enter back into God's Heart, into Heaven, and complete our journey.

The Spark of Divinity,
The Power of God,
Will emancipate mankind,
Rejuvenating us into a beautiful, joyful world,
Full of inspiration and conviction,
Motivating us,
To understand one another,
To unwind the deeds of our ego,
To cut the strings of falsehood and illusion,
To feel the rain of joy,
Dancing on the streets,
In a cascade of Divine Vibrations.
Knowing and wanting
To feel the crispness of a winter frost,
The brightness of a blue sky,
The warmth of the shimmering sun.
I long for the day,
That we may pray together, as one,
Feasting for eternity upon The Love of God.

The Divine Mother flies out through the French windows and beckons me to go with Mother, to hold Mother's Hand. So now you see – The Spirit can really fly.

Printed in Great Britain
by Amazon

19919149R00037